LUXOR, KARNAK, AND THE THEBAN TE

EGYPT POCKET GUIDE

Alberto Siliotti

THE AMERICAN UNIVERSITY IN CAIRO PRESS

Text and Photographs Alberto Siliotti
Drawings Melissa Frigotto, Jean-Claude Golvin
English Translation Richard Pierce

General Editing Yvonne Marzoni
Graphic Design Geodia

Copyright © 2002 by Geodia (Verona, Italy)

This edition first published in Egypt jointly by
The American University in Cairo Press (Cairo and New York)
Elias Modern Publishing House (Cairo)
Geodia (Verona, Italy)
Second printing 2005

Created by Geodia (Verona, Italy)
Printed in Egypt by Elias Modern Publishing House (Cairo)
Distributed by the American University in Cairo Press (Cairo and New York)

ISBN 977 424 641 1

Dar El Kutub 17880/00

In the text "(⇨ X)" means "go to page X"

Contents

The temple of Hatshepsut at Deir al-Bahari

INTRODUCTION

Chronological table 4
Luxor, Ancient Thebes 5
Reconstruction of Thebes 6
- The Feast of the Valley 7

LUXOR

The Temple of Luxor 8
- The Luxor Cachette 13
The Avenue of the Sphinxes 14

Temple of Amun-Re, Karnak

KARNAK

Karnak and Its Temples 15
Plan of the Temple of Amun-Re 16
- The Temple
of Amun-Re in Figures 18
Three-dimensional Representation
of the Temple of Amun-Re 18
- The Karnak Cachette 20
Open-air museum 25
The Feast of Opet 26

WEST THEBES

The Colossi of Memnon 27

Medinet Habu 29
- The Sea Peoples 31
The Ramesseum 32
The Deir al-Bahari Complex 34
- The Mysterious Land of Punt 36
The Temple of Sethos I 38

THE MUSEUMS

The Museum of Luxor 40
The Mummification
Museum 44

DENDERA

The Temple of Dendera 46

BIBLIOGRAPHY 48

The Temple of Luxor

Temple of Luxor, the solar court of Amenophis III

CHRONOLOGICAL TABLE

2670 B.C. - 2150 B.C.	**OLD KINGDOM**
2150 B.C. - 2056 B.C.	**FIRST INTERMEDIATE PERIOD**
2056 B.C. - 1650 B.C.	**MIDDLE KINGDOM**
1650 B.C. - 1550 B.C.	**SECOND INTERMEDIATE PERIOD**
1550 B.C. - 1076 B.C.	**NEW KINGDOM**

18th DYNASTY 1550 B.C.-1295 B.C.

Ahmose	1550 - 1525
Amenophis I	1525 - 1504
Tuthmosis I	1504 - 1492
Tuthmosis II	1492 - 1479
Hatshepsut	1479 - 1457
Tuthmosis III	1479 - 1425
Amenophis II	1427 - 1397
Tuthmosis IV	1397 - 1387
Amenophis III	1387 - 1349
Amenophis IV / Akhenaten	1349 - 1333
Smenkhkare	1335 - 1333
Tutankhamun	1333 - 1324
Ay	1324 - 1321
Haremhab	1321 - 1295

19th DYNASTY 1295 B.C.-1188 B.C.

Ramesses I	1295 - 1294
Sethos I	1294 - 1279
Ramesses II	1279 - 1213
Merneptah	1213 - 1204
Amenmesse	1204 - 1201
Sethos II	1201 - 1195
Siptah	1195 - 1190
Tworse	1190 - 1188

20th DYNASTY 1188 B.C.-1076 B.C.

Sethnakhte	1188 - 1186
Ramesses III	1186 - 1154
Ramesses IV	1154 - 1148
Ramesses V	1148 - 1144
Ramesses VI	1144 - 1136
Ramesses VII	1136 - 1128
Ramesses VIII	1128 - 1125
Ramesses IX	1125 - 1107
Ramesses X	1107 - 1089
Ramesses XI	1098 - 1076

1076 B.C. - 712 B.C.	**THIRD INTERMEDIATE PERIOD**
712 B.C. - 332 B.C.	**LATE PERIOD**
332 B.C. - 395 A.D.	**GRECO-ROMAN PERIOD**

Hieroglyph of the place-name Waset

Luxor, Ancient Thebes

*T*he area comprising the present-day town of Luxor and the site of Karnak corresponds to ancient Thebes, the great capital of Egypt during the New Kingdom.

Personification of the Theban nome in one of the triads of Menkaure (Egyptian Museum, Cairo)

*View of the Karnak area and the Temple of Mut (**M**)*

Homer used the word "Thebes" to indicate the ancient capital of Egypt, which was originally called Waset, "the city of the *was* scepter," like the fourth nome in Upper Egypt of which it was a part. In Book IX of the *Iliad* the great Greek poet called it "Thebes of a hundred gates," and here the word "gate" means the entrances to the temples, not only those in the city walls. It is not clear why the Greeks used the name Thebes for Waset, as it was already the name of the city in Boeotia, but it may have been due to the similar sound of the two names. Waset was the name of the city proper on the east bank of the Nile (East Thebes) as well as of the necropolis that lay on the opposite side (West Thebes). The rise of Thebes began in the Middle Kingdom, around 2056 BC, but the city only became the capital of Egypt after the Hyksos invaders were driven out of the country at the beginning of the New Kingdom, in 1550 BC. The chief Theban deity was Amun, "He who is hidden," who was part of the Theban triad together with his wife Mut and son Khons.

The god Amun (Museum of Ancient Egyptian Art, Luxor)

6

Temple of Ay and Haremheb

Temple of Amenophis III

Temple of Tuthmosis IV

Temple of Ramesses III

Temple of Merneptah

Temple of Ramesses II (Ramesseum)

Temple of Luxor

Avenue of Sphinxes

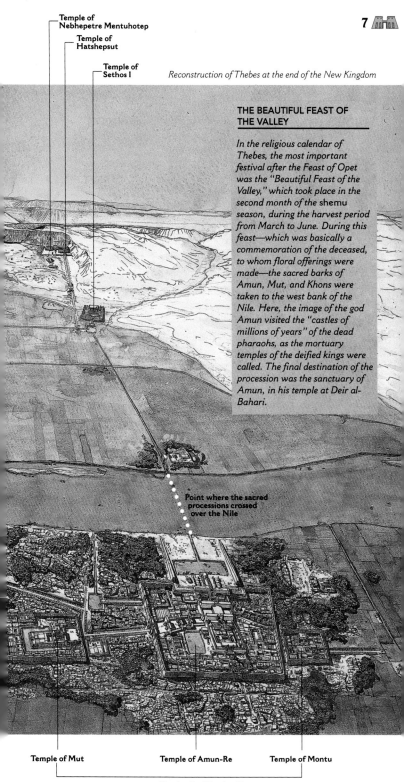

Temple of
Nebhepetre Mentuhotep

Temple of
Hatshepsut

Temple of
Sethos I

Reconstruction of Thebes at the end of the New Kingdom

THE BEAUTIFUL FEAST OF THE VALLEY

In the religious calendar of Thebes, the most important festival after the Feast of Opet was the "Beautiful Feast of the Valley," which took place in the second month of the shemu season, during the harvest period from March to June. During this feast—which was basically a commemoration of the deceased, to whom floral offerings were made—the sacred barks of Amun, Mut, and Khons were taken to the west bank of the Nile. Here, the image of the god Amun visited the "castles of millions of years" of the dead pharaohs, as the mortuary temples of the deified kings were called. The final destination of the procession was the sanctuary of Amun, in his temple at Deir al-Bahari.

Point where the sacred
processions crossed
over the Nile

Temple of Mut

Temple of Amun-Re

Temple of Montu

K A R N A K

The Temple of Luxor

Situated in the heart of the present-day town, the Temple of Luxor, known as the "southern harem of Amun," was the venue for complex liturgical rites.

The name of the present-day town of Luxor derives from the Arabic al-uqsor, the plural of al-qasr, the "camp," since in the 3rd century AD it was the site of a fortified Roman camp or castrum. The temple was originally called Ipet resyt en Imen, "the southern harem of Amun," which was the residence of a particular form of the god Amun known as Amenemope, or "Amun in Opet," which was visited

The western obelisk at Luxor, now in the Place de la Concorde, Paris

The pylon of Ramesses II, with the eastern obelisk (25 meters tall), and the two colossi of the king seated on his throne

by the image of Amun of Karnak once a year during the Feast of Opet, a series of ceremonies connected to the regeneration of royal power. The core of the Temple of Luxor was built by Amenophis III (also known as Amenhotep III), who reigned from 1387–1349 BC, but the construction as we see it now was the work of Ramesses II (1279–1213 BC), who added another

court and a pylon to the great colonnade. However, the axis of Ramesses' court was not aligned with the

The first court of the Temple of Luxor seen from the east

pre-existing architectural elements, but rather with the junction point of the processional avenues of Mut and Khons at Karnak. Two colossi of Ramesses II and two obelisks preceded the pylon: the obelisks were donated to France in 1830 by the pasha of Egypt, Muhammed Ali, but only

The triple chapel of Hatshepsut, which was rebuilt by Ramesses II, lies against the inner side of the pylon

One of the two colossi of Ramesses II on his throne in the first court

quay is the triple shrine for the barks of Amun, Mut, and Khons, which is decorated by four elegant papyrus bundle columns

and was rebuilt by Ramesses II over a previous structure dating from Hatshepsut's reign. Ramesses II's courtyard is

the western one, which is 22.83 meters high, was actually taken to France and set up in Place de la Concorde in Paris in 1836. The pylon is decorated on the outer side with representations of the Battle of Qadesh, while on the inner side of the west

Plan of the Temple of Luxor

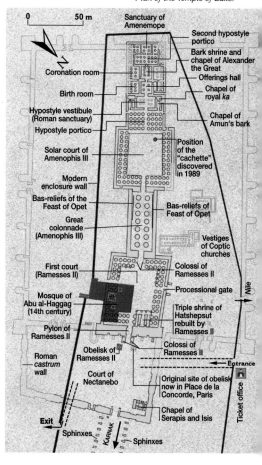

Plan labels:
- 0 — 50 m
- Sanctuary of Amenemope
- Second hypostyle portico
- Bark shrine and chapel of Alexander the Great
- Coronation room
- Offerings hall
- Chapel of royal ka
- Birth room
- Hypostyle vestibule (Roman sanctuary)
- Chapel of Amun's bark
- Hypostyle portico
- Solar court of Amenophis III
- Position of the "cachette" discovered in 1989
- Modern enclosure wall
- Bas-reliefs of the Feast of Opet
- Bas-reliefs of Feast of Opet
- Great colonnade (Amenophis III)
- Vestiges of Coptic churches
- First court (Ramesses II)
- Colossi of Ramesses II
- Mosque of Abu al-Haggag (14th century)
- Processional gate
- Triple shrine of Hatshepsut rebuilt by Ramesses II
- Pylon of Ramesses II
- Colossi of Ramesses II
- Roman castrum wall
- Obelisk of Ramesses II
- Original site of obelisk now in Place de la Concorde, Paris
- Court of Nectanebo
- Entrance
- Chapel of Serapis and Isis
- Ticket office
- Nile
- Exit
- Sphinxes
- KARNAK
- Sphinxes

The so-called "Roman sanctuary," decorated with an apse with two Corinthian columns. This was the religious center of the Roman castrum

The hypostyle portico with papyrus-bundle columns and, in the background, the apse of the "Roman sanctuary"

The mosque of Abu al-Haggag viewed from the court of Ramesses II

Roman sanctuary

Hypostyle portico

Solar court of Amenophis III

Great colonnade of Amenophis III

First court (Ramesses II)

Mosque of Abu al-Haggag

Entrance to the Mosque of Abu al-Haggag (14th century)

decorated on three sides by 74 papyrus columns with closed capitals laid out in double rows and with statues of the pharaoh between them. Ramesses II is depicted in the act of marching with the mekes papyrus scroll, the emblem of transmitted royal power, in his hand; he is

Statue of Ramesses II in the first courtyard

accompanied by his consort Nefertari, who is sculpted next to his knee. The colonnade is interrupted on the eastern side because it was covered in the 14th century by the mosque built in honor of Abu al-Haggag, a holy man venerated in this region who died in 1244 AD. Two colossal statues of Ramesses II on his throne afford access to the imposing colonnade of Amenophis III, which consists of 14 papyrus columns, each 19 meters tall with open umbel capitals. The walls delimiting the colonnade to the east and west are decorated with bas-reliefs illustrating the Feast of

Nefertari depicted next to the knee of one of the statues of Ramesses II (first courtyard)

Opet and date from the reign of Tutankhamun (1333–1324 BC). On the west side is the procession from Karnak to Luxor, while the east side has a representation of the

Chapel of Serapis and Isis

return to Karnak. Again dating back to Tutankhamun's time are two statue groups in the first part of the colonnade that depict Amun with the pharaoh's features and accompanied by the goddess Mut. The large colonnade gives access to

The two colossi of Ramesses II in front of the pylon

Pylon of Ramesses II

Colossi of Ramesses II

Obelisk of Ramesses II

Original site of the obelisk now in Paris

Entrance

Ticket office

Chapel of Serapis and Isis (Hadrian's era)

Sphinxes

KARNAK

Avenue of sphinxes

Sphinxes

The great colonnade of Amenophis III, originally covered with limestone slabs

The white limestone double-statue of the gods Amun and Mut in the great colonnade of Amenophis III

the solar court of Amenophis III, which also has a peristyle, and is bordered on three sides by a double row of papyrus-bundle columns. This large space was the venue for the ritual of the Feast of Opet, where the sacred barks of Amun, Mut, and Khons were acclaimed and worshipped before being

The hypostyle portico, the solar court of Amenophis III and the great colonnade in an aerial view

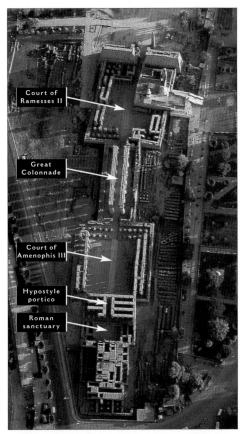

Court of
Ramesses II

Great
Colonnade

Court of
Amenophis III

Hypostyle
portico

Roman
sanctuary

transported to the innermost part of the temple, which began with the hypostyle hall. This latter is supported by 32 payrus-bundle columns and is also the southern side of the solar court. It gives access to the first hypostyle vestibule known as the "Roman sanctuary," so called because it was transformed into a sanctuary by the emperor Diocletian's legionaries, who bricked up the large door to the innermost part of the temple in the 3rd century AD, thus creating an apse. To this day, to penetrate the second vestibule with four columns known as the "offerings hall" one must pass through a narrow opening in the Roman wall. By proceeding along the axis of the temple one arrives at the "shrine of

*Aerial view of the
Temple of Luxor*

The scene of the divine marriage depicted in the birth room.

The birth room seen from the east

Amun's bark," where the god's bark was laid. This area was later occupied by the shrine that Alexander the Great (356–323 BC) had built, which is still standing. Past a second hypostyle portico is the last part of the temple, consisting of the sanctuary of Amun, constructed during the reign of Amenophis III, which is flanked by two chapels. This was the "home" of the statue of Amun of Luxor (Amenemope), which was visited every year by the image of Amun of Karnak in order to be regenerated. The second part of this ritual took place in the birth room, situated

The sanctuary of Amun

immediately east of the offerings antechamber. This is decorated with reliefs depicting the divine union of the queen Mutemwiya with the god Amun in the guise of her terrestrial husband Tuthmosis IV to generate Amenophis IV,

under the auspices of the goddesses Selket and Neith. It was in this chamber that the regeneration of royal power took place; indeed, the royal function was not only revitalized but also sanctioned.

THE LUXOR CACHETTE

The deep pit that contained the statues

On January 23, 1989 the Egyptian press printed the official announcement that during work carried out to ascertain the stability of the columns in the Temple of Luxor, a perfectly intact statue of the pharaoh Amenophis III had been found. Actually, this discovery not only concerned a statue, but an entire cache—called "cachette" after a term used by French archaeologists—where the priests had deposited numerous statues because of lack of space or for other unknown reasons. The excavations carried out in the following months brought to light 22 statues, the most recent of which dated back to the 25th Dynasty, that is, a period between the 8th and 7th century BC.

The large statue of Amenophis III, now in the Luxor museum, a few days after it was discovered

The Avenue of Sphinxes

A long avenue of sphinxes connected the Temple of Luxor and the Temple of Karnak about three kilometers away.

One of the human-headed sphinxes of Nectanebo I

The avenue of sphinxes, built during the reign of Nectanebo I

I n front of the pylon of Ramesses II in the temple of Luxor, Nectanebo I (380–362 BC) built a courtyard which was the starting point of a long avenue to Karnak— also named *dromos* from the Greek—that was lined by a double row of sphinxes with human heads and lions' bodies. Archaeologists think this causeway had 730 (2 x 365) sphinxes, 58 of which are still standing. This processional route, which already existed in Hatshepsut's time (1479–1457 BC), was used as part of the land itinerary of the Feast of Opet (⇨ **26**) when the procession started off from Karnak for Luxor.

Other processional routes with criosphinxes (sphinxes with lions' bodies and rams' heads) connected the Temple of Mut and the tenth pylon of Karnak, and the Temple of Amun-Re at the quay: this latter avenue, which dates from the time of Ramesses II, probably began at the second pylon of the Temple of Karnak. An avenue with statues of rams (with a ram's head and body) dating from the reign of Amenophis III linked the Temple of Khons and the platform, situated 176 meters from the gate of Euergetes, from where the processional avenue to Luxor began.

The complex network of processional avenues

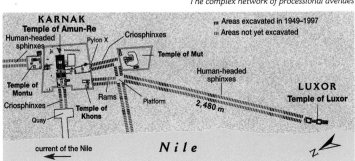

KARNAK
Temple of Amun-Re
Human-headed sphinxes
Pylon X
Criosphinxes
Temple of Mut
Human-headed sphinxes
Temple of Montu
Criosphinxes
Rams
Temple of Khons
Platform
Quay
2,480 m
LUXOR
Temple of Luxor

ᵢᵢᵢ Areas excavated in 1949–1997
ᵢᵢᵢ Areas not yet excavated

current of the Nile   *N i l e*

Karnak and Its Temples

*K*arnak was the largest and most impressive religious center in ancient Egypt, with 2,000 years of history: a monumental complex in the middle of which stood the Temple of Amun-Re, the king of the gods.

The god Amun-Re

Pylon I of the Temple of Karnak was left unfinished

*K*arnak, the Arabic name of a nearby village that means "fortified wall," was the center of

A ram-headed sphinx (criosphinx) in the avenue that connected pylon I and the quay

the religious and economic life of Egypt during the New Kingdom. The huge size of the Temple of Amun-Re, the original name of which was *Ipet-sut*, "the most venerated of the places [of Amun]," is the result of enlargement and beautification works carried out in a period of over 2,000 years. In fact, there was no pharaoh who did not want to leave a tangible sign of his reign at Karnak. Amun, the "unknowable," the king of the gods whose cult had supplanted that of Montu, the local god of

war to whom was dedicated a temple immediately north of the Temple of Amun, was the lord of Karnak. He was associated in a triad with his consort Mut, to whom another temple south of

The gods Amun, Mut, and Khons, the Theban triad

Plan of the Temple of

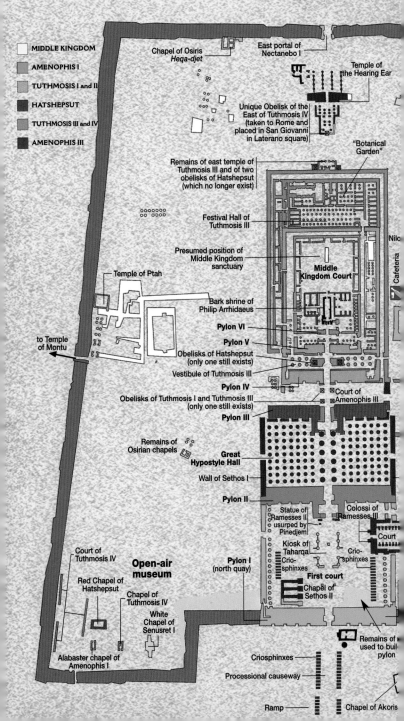

MIDDLE KINGDOM

AMENOPHIS I

TUTHMOSIS I and II

HATSHEPSUT

TUTHMOSIS III and IV

AMENOPHIS III

Chapel of Osiris
Heqa-djet

East portal of
Nectanebo I

Temple of
the Hearing Ear

Unique Obelisk of the
East of Tuthmosis IV
(taken to Rome and
placed in San Giovanni
in Laterano square)

"Botanical
Garden"

Remains of east temple of
Tuthmosis III and of two
obelisks of Hatshepsut
(which no longer exist)

Festival Hall of
Tuthmosis III

Nilo

Cafeteria

Presumed position of
Middle Kingdom
sanctuary

Middle
Kingdom Court

Temple of Ptah

Bark shrine of
Philip Arrhidaeus

to Temple
of Montu

Pylon VI

Pylon V

Obelisks of Hatshepsut
(only one still exists)

Vestibule of Tuthmosis III

Pylon IV

Court of
Amenophis III

Obelisk of Tuthmosis I and Tuthmosis III
(only one still exists)

Pylon III

Remains of
Osirian chapels

Great
Hypostyle Hall

Wall of Sethos I

Pylon II

Statue of
Ramesses II
usurped by
Pinedjem

Colossi of
Ramesses III

Court

Kiosk of
Taharqa
Crio-
sphinxes

Crio-
sphinxes

Court of
Tuthmosis IV

Open-air
museum

Pylon I
(north quay)

First court

Chapel of
Sethos II

Red Chapel of
Hatshepsut

Chapel of
Tuthmosis IV

White
Chapel of
Senusret I

Remains of
used to buil
pylon

Alabaster chapel of
Amenophis I

Criosphinxes

Processional causeway

Ramp

Chapel of Akoris

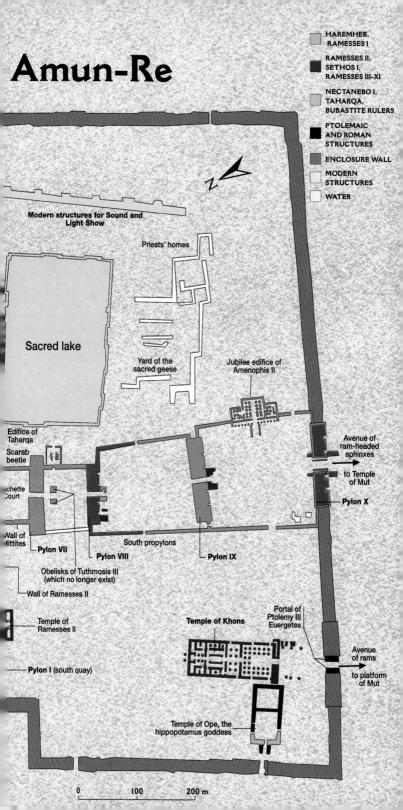

Amun-Re

HAREMHEB,
RAMESSES I

RAMESSES II,
SETHOS I,
RAMESSES III-XI

NECTANEBO I,
TAHARQA,
BUBASTITE RULERS

PTOLEMAIC
AND ROMAN
STRUCTURES

ENCLOSURE WALL

MODERN
STRUCTURES

WATER

N

Modern structures for Sound and
Light Show

Priests' homes

Sacred lake

Yard of the
sacred geese

Jubilee edifice of
Amenophis II

Edifice of
Taharqa

Scarab
beetle

Avenue of
ram-headed
sphinxes

to Temple
of Mut

Pylon X

chette
Court

Wall of
Hittites

Pylon VII

Pylon VIII

South propylons

Pylon IX

Obelisks of Tuthmosis III
(which no longer exist)

Wall of Ramesses II

Temple of
Ramesses II

Portal of
Ptolemy III
Euergetes

Temple of Khons

Pylon I (south quay)

Avenue
of rams

to platform
of Mut

Temple of Ope, the
hippopotamus goddess

0   100   200 m

Amun's was dedicated, and their son Khons.

The original core of the Temple of Amun dates from the Middle Kingdom, when Senusret I (1964–1919 BC) built the first shrine for the statue of Amun and also built, in an area called the Middle Kingdom Court, a white, Tura limestone shrine known as the White Chapel (⇨ 25), the only vestige of this period. At the beginning of the 18th Dynasty, Amenophis I (1525–1504 BC) commissioned the construction, in the Middle Kingdom Court, of the first bark chapel of Amun, which was decorated with jubilee scenes; but it was

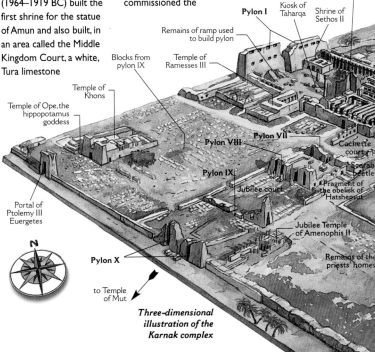

Pylon I
Kiosk of Taharqa
Shrine of Sethos II
Pylon II
Remains of ramp used to build pylon
Blocks from pylon IX
Temple of Ramesses III
Temple of Khons
Temple of Ope, the hippopotamus goddess
Pylon VIII
Pylon VII
Cachette court
Scarab beetle
Pylon IX
Fragment of the obelisk of Hatshepsut
Jubilee court
Jubilee Temple of Amenophis II
Portal of Ptolemy III Euergetes
Remains of the priests' homes
Pylon X
N
to Temple of Mut

Three-dimensional illustration of the Karnak complex

THE TEMPLE OF AMUN-RE IN FIGURES

Total surface area: about 300,000 m²
Perimeter of the Amun-Re enclosure: 2,260 m
Max. length of the temple (E-W axis): 150 m
Max. length of the temple (N-S axis): about 100 m

Surface area of hypostyle hall: 5,300 m²
Columns in hypostyle hall: 134
Max. height of hypostyle hall columns (central columns): 21 m
Max. height of pylons (II and X): 35 m
Height of obelisk of Hatshepsut: 28.5 m
Weight of obelisk of Hatshepsut: 325 tons
Height of obelisk of Tuthmosis I: 19.5 m
Weight of obelisk of Tuthmosis I: 120 tons
Surface area of sacred lake: 9,250 m²

Average annual number of flower offerings: 1,656,120
Staff working on Amun's sacred sites at Karnak during the reign of Ramesses III: 81,322 persons

Pylon VI and the bark shrine of Amun built by Philip Arrhidaeus, successor to Alexander the Great, on the site where Tuthmosis III's shrine once stood

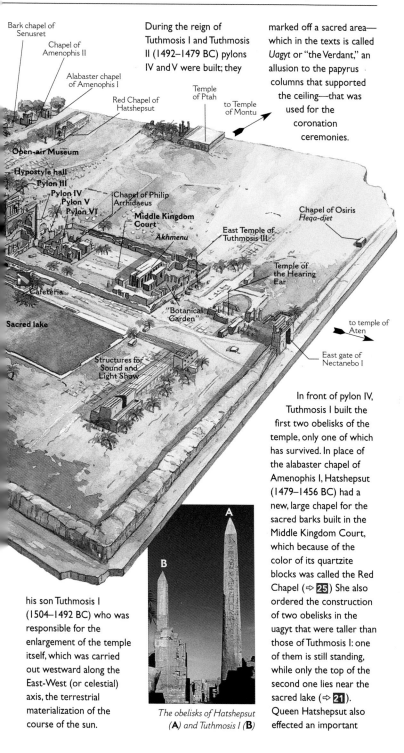

Bark chapel of Senusret
Chapel of Amenophis II
Alabaster chapel of Amenophis I
Red Chapel of Hatshepsut
Temple of Ptah
to Temple of Montu
Open-air Museum
Hypostyle hall
Pylon III
Pylon IV
Pylon V
Pylon VI
Chapel of Philip Arrhidaeus
Middle Kingdom Court
Akhmenu
East Temple of Tuthmosis III
Chapel of Osiris *Heqa-djet*
Cafeteria
Temple of the Hearing Ear
Sacred lake
"Botanical Garden"
to temple of Aten
East gate of Nectanebo I
Structures for Sound and Light Show

During the reign of Tuthmosis I and Tuthmosis II (1492–1479 BC) pylons IV and V were built; they marked off a sacred area— which in the texts is called *Uagyt* or "the Verdant," an allusion to the papyrus columns that supported the ceiling—that was used for the coronation ceremonies.

his son Tuthmosis I (1504–1492 BC) who was responsible for the enlargement of the temple itself, which was carried out westward along the East-West (or celestial) axis, the terrestrial materialization of the course of the sun.

The obelisks of Hatshepsut (A) and Tuthmosis I (B)

In front of pylon IV, Tuthmosis I built the first two obelisks of the temple, only one of which has survived. In place of the alabaster chapel of Amenophis I, Hatshepsut (1479–1456 BC) had a new, large chapel for the sacred barks built in the Middle Kingdom Court, which because of the color of its quartzite blocks was called the Red Chapel (⇨ 25) She also ordered the construction of two obelisks in the uagyt that were taller than those of Tuthmosis I: one of them is still standing, while only the top of the second one lies near the sacred lake (⇨ 21). Queen Hatshepsut also effected an important

Pylon VIII and, in the background, the obelisks of Hatshepsut and Tuthmosis I

THE KARNAK CACHETTE

In 1903, in the court opposite pylon VII, the French archaeologist Georges Legrain discovered a cache (or "cachette" in French) in which the Egyptian priests had buried an extraordinary number of statues: the digs brought to light 20,000 finds, including 900 stone statues. Since that time the area has been known as the "Cachette Court."

change in the history of the Temple of Amun-Re because of the construction of pylon VIII, which led to the development of a new North-South axis parallel to the Nile that symbolized the terrestrial axis and was related to royal power, crossing the original East-West axis of the temple in front of pylon IV. During the reign of Tuthmosis III (1479–1425 BC), the nephew and stepson of Hatshepsut, called the "Egyptian Napoleon," the enlargement works on the temple went along at an

extraordinary pace. This pharaoh had a new pylon built, the seventh, in front of Hatshepsut's, preceded by two obelisks, one of which, around 330 AD

Bas-relief in the "Botanical Garden"

during the age of Constantine, was taken to Constantinople (present-day Istanbul), where it still stands. Tuthmosis III also had two other obelisks (which no longer exist) built immediately west of Tuthmosis II's: the presence of four obelisks thus marked the meeting of the four cardinal points of the kingdom of Amun-Re, of whom the pharaoh was the divine son and

The Akhmenu of Tuthmosis III and the Festival Hall

One of the tent-pole columns in the Festival Hall

"tent poles" in that they reproduce the pole of the tents originally used to celebrate the early jubilee feasts in honor of the king. The Festival Temple also has the so-called Botanical Garden, so named because the bas-reliefs that decorate its walls depict

primeval marsh from which the world was born, and it also served as a reservoir (26,000 cubic meters)

The top of the second obelisk of Hatshepsut near the Sacred Lake

representative on Earth. Furthermore, on the eastern side of the Middle Kingdom Court, Tuthmosis III built a unique monumental complex called *Akhmenu*, or the

The Sacred Lake and, in the background, the Akhmenu *(A), the Temple of the Hearing Ear (B), and the east gate (C).*

"Most Splendid of Monuments," which was basically a shrine connected to the celebration of royal power in conjunction with the divine power of Amun-Re. The central section of the Akhmenu consists of a jubilee hall, the Festival Temple, which is entirely decorated and painted and the ceiling of which is supported by specially-shaped columns known as

plants and animals of the Asian regions where Tuthmosis III waged many military campaigns. South of the Festival Temple is the large Sacred Lake, which has a two-fold symbolic and practical function: it evoked *Nun*, the

The famous scarab beetle, an image of Khepri, the dawn form of the sun god Ra, which came from the Temple of Amenophis III at West Thebes

thanks to the water table beneath it, as a place for ablutions, rituals, and the material needs of the priests whose residential quarters lay on the southern side of the lake. The area opposite the north bank of the basin and parallel to the south side of the Temple of Amun, decorated with liturgic and offering scenes, was on the other hand a sacred precinct in which, during the 25th Ethiopian Dynasty, the pharaoh Taharqa (690–664 BC) built a sanctuary, the foundations of which are still standing. This enclosure was used to celebrate the mystery of the creation of the world by Amun-Re; this is probably the reason why the sacred scarab beetle, which was originally in the Temple of Amenophis III at West Thebes, was brought here. Certainly the most impressive part of the Temple of Amun is the hypostyle hall, an immense structure of 5,300 square meters built under the reigns of Sethos I (1321–1295 BC) and Ramesses II (1279–1231 BC) between pylon III of Amenophis III (1387–1349 BC) and pylon II of Haremheb (1321–1295 BC). It is divided into two sections (northern and southern) by the central nave which is supported by twelve columns, each 22.4 meters tall. One hundred and twenty-two papyriform columns with closed capitals, symbolizing the primeval papyrus marsh, line the pavement of the hypostyle hall north and south of the nave itself. The spaces between these columns were originally occupied by statues of divinities and pharaohs, some of which have recently been put back in place. Besides the cartouches, many of the columns have a great

Bas-relief in the hypostyle hall: transporting Amun's sacred bark for the Feast of Opet

The imposing columns in the hypostyle hall are 22.5 meters high; the arrow indicates one of the claustra, *openings through which light penetrated the interior*

number of carvings of the *rekhyt* bird, the plover which symbolized the union of the king and his people and at the same time marked out the public areas of the temple. In this hall used to celebrate the pharaoh's regality—the construction of which began with Sethos I and was completed by his son Ramesses II—the bas-reliefs on the walls illustrate the two main feasts of the Theban liturgical year, the Feast of Opet and the Beautiful Feast of the Valley, as well as the coronation

The rekhyt *plover*

*The first court with pylon II (**A**), the Kiosk of Taharqa (**B**), and the Temple of Ramesses III (**C**)*

ceremonies represented on the west wall. The first court is the first area the visitor enters after having passed through the huge

The Chapel of Sethos II

first pylon, attributed to Nectanebo I (378–360 BC). This court is bounded to the east by pylon II and to the north by a portico built during the 22nd Dynasty, called the Bubastite Portico by Champollion in reference to the city of Bubastis in the Nile Delta that was the capital of Egypt in

The statue of Ramesses II and Nefertari

that period. The northwestern corner of the court is occupied by the tripartite shrine for the barks of Amun, Mut, and Khons, built by Sethos II (1201–1195 BC). This is preceded by an altar on which Amun-Re's bark was placed. In the middle of the courtyard are the remains of the kiosk of the pharaoh Taharqa, the only standing part of which is a 21–meter column. Opposite the column is a colossal red granite statue 15 meters high depicting Ramesses II with his consort Nefertari standing between his knees which was usurped by the high priest Pinedjem (1070–1032 BC). The statue was

Reconstruction of the Kiosk of Taharqa

later found near pylon II and placed in its present position in the early 20th century. On the south side of the court is the Temple of Ramesses III (1186–1154 BC), whose structure seems to be a miniature version of the royal cult temple of this pharaoh at Medinet Habu (⇒ **29**).

The Temple of Ramesses III

The Temple of Khons

The Southern Area

In the southern area of the precint of Amun is the **Temple of Khons**, a god connected to lunar cults and considered the son of Amun-Re. This edifice, built during the reign of Ramesses III, is the only temple at Karnak that is almost intact and therefore clearly illustrates what an ancient Egyptian temple looked like. Several of the bas-reliefs that decorate the inside walls, many of which were executed in the Ptolemaic period, have preserved their original colors. South of the temple is the impressive **portal built by Ptolemy III Euergetes** (246–221 BC), decorated with exquisite bas-reliefs and surmounted by the ogee molding typical of the Ptolemaic period. Beyond

Ptolemy III Euergetes' portal

the portal is an **avenue of ram statues** that is connected to the one from the Temple of Mut in a kind of platform.

The Northern Area

In the northern sector, the most interesting monument is the small but well-preserved **Temple of Ptah**, which lies against both the Temple of Amun precinct and the Temple of Montu precinct. This

The lion-headed goddess Sekhmet in the Temple of Ptah

temple, which was also connected to the coronation rituals, was dedicated to the chief divinity of Memphis, the historic capital of Egypt during the Old Kingdom, where the first pharaoh of Egypt was presumedly crowned. In one of the three chapels that form the innermost part, beyond a small pylon, is a fine statue of the lion-headed goddess Sekhmet, the protectress of royal power and consort of Ptah.

The Temple of the Hearing Ear built by Ramesses II

The Eastern Area

This sector, which lies against the Akhmenu, contains the remains of the eastern **temple of Tuthmosis III** which incorporated two obelisks built by Hatshepsut (that no longer exist). In a much better state of preservation is a **Temple** of Ramesses II, that constitutes the east end of the Amun precinct and was **dedicated to "the Hearing Ear,"** a popular form of Amun. This temple incorporated the largest of all the obelisks in Egypt, known as the "Unique Obelisk of the East," which was erected by Tuthmosis IV and was taken to Rome during the reign of Constantine, around 330 AD. Farther north is the Osirian sector of the temple, the only monument of which that can be seen today is the small **chapel of Osiris Heqa-djet.**

33,10 m

The Unique Obelisk of the East, now at San Giovanni in Laterano, Rome

The Open-air Museum

*T*he open-air museum, situated in the northwestern area of the Temple of Karnak, has three important chapels decorated with bas-reliefs of great artistic and historic value.

Senusret I

The White Chapel of Senusret I

There are some very interesting monuments in the open-air museum. The pride and joy of the museum is the **White**

The Alabaster Chapel of Amenophis I

Chapel of Senusret I (1964–1919 BC), whose bas-reliefs are a masterpiece of Middle Kingdom sculpture. This jubilee kiosk, used for the feast of the ithyphallic god Min, is the oldest monument in Karnak and was found dismantled inside pylon III in 1927 and was then reconstructed in its present position.

A few dozen meters away is the **Red Chapel of**

Hatshepsut (1479–1457 BC), the 300 or so red quartzite and diorite blocks of which had been laid out in long rows in the same area; it was reassembled in 2000 by the Franco-Egyptian Center for the Studies of the Karnak Temples. Scholars believe that this building, used as a station for Amun's bark, originally stood on the site where the chapel of Philip Arrhidaeus was later built. Another treasure in the museum is the **Alabaster Chapel of Amenophis I** (1515–1504 BC), which is flanked by another chapel similar to the one built during the reign of Tuthmosis IV.

The Red Chapel of Hatshepsut, rebuilt in 2000

The Feast of Opet

*T*his was the most important religious festival in Thebes, during which the image of the god Amun of Karnak was carried to the Temple of Luxor in a grand procession.

Trumpeters announce the procession

Priests transporting the bark of Khons

*T*he complex liturgical calendar in ancient Egypt contained numerous feasts, the most important of which, during the New Kingdom, was the Feast of Opet or Feast of the Harem, which took place in the second month of the flood season (*akhet*),

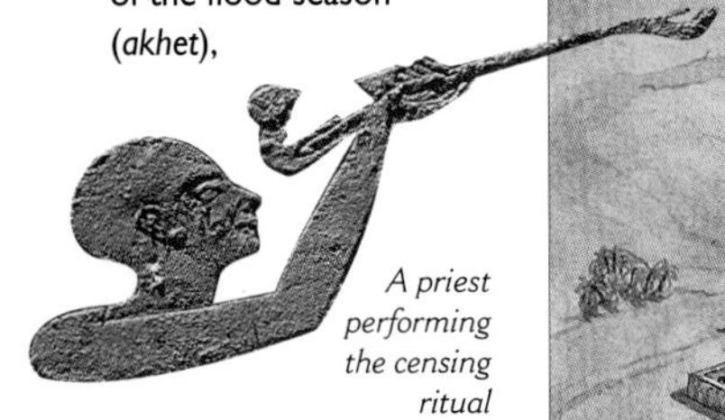

A priest performing the censing ritual

which was later called *Paofi*, or "the month of Opet." During this solemn feast there was a grand procession in which the simulacra of the sacred barks of Amun, Mut, and Khons were borne to the Temple of Luxor along the large avenue of sphinxes that connected

Temple of Amun-Re

Temple of Montu

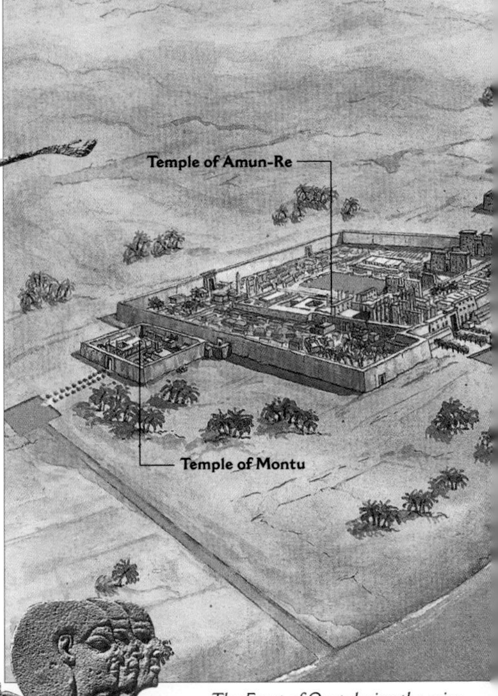

The Feast of Opet during the reign of Amenophis III

Musicians playing the lute

the two temples, while the people cheered during the entire procession. At the end of the ceremonies, which during the reign of Tuthmosis III lasted eleven days, the procession went down the Nile on boats to return to Karnak. Later on, from the reign of Amenophis III onward, the procession went to Luxor by going up the Nile and then returned to Karnak on land. The details of the

A priest about to sacrifice bulls and oxen

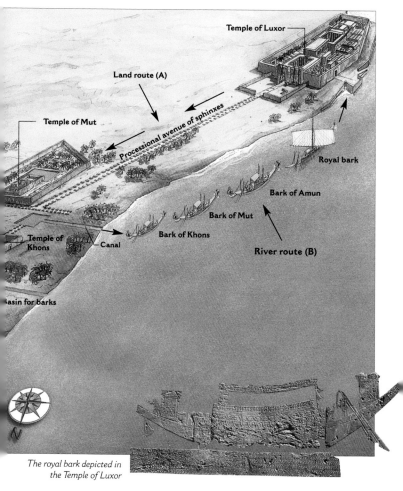

The royal bark depicted in the Temple of Luxor

Feast of Opet are illustrated in the bas-reliefs that decorate the walls flanking the Great Colonnade of the Temple of Luxor, which were executed during Tutankhamun's time (1333–1324 BC).

The Colossi of Memnon

Colossal head of Amenophis III found at Kom al-Hetan

*T*he two gigantic, solitary statues that welcome visitors to West Thebes at Kom al-Hetan, are all that remains of the Temple of Amenophis III, the largest Theban temple.

The two colossal statues, which originally stood in front of the first pylon of the Temple of Amenophis III

*D*espite its huge size, almost nothing remains of the Temple of Amenophis III except for the two 17–meter colossi that stood before the first pylon and represented the pharaoh flanked by his mother Mutemwiya (left) and his consort Tiy (right). Built of mud bricks and not in blocks of cut stone as was common in the 19th Dynasty, and too close to the Nile, the Temple of Amenophis III soon deteriorated, and already during the Roman period the only remains were the two colossi, which soon became a popular sight because of a strange phenomenon. One of the two statues, the northern one, made a sound at dawn that the ancient Greeks interpreted as the lament of the Homeric hero Memnon—with whom the colossus was identified, perhaps because of a phonetic similarity between the names Memnon and Amenophis—to his mother Dawn. The sound, really caused by the air warmed by the sun passing through a crack in the statue, was attested to by hundreds of inscriptions.

It disappeared after the monument was restored by Septimius Severus in the 2nd century AD.

Plan of the Temple of Amenophis III at Kom al-Hetan

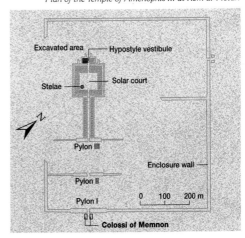

Excavated area — Hypostyle vestibule

Stelae — Solar court

Pylon III

Enclosure wall

Pylon II

Pylon I

0   100   200 m

Colossi of Memnon

Medinet Habu

The Temple of Ramesses III at Medinet Habu, an enlarged version of the Ramesseum, is the best-preserved Theban monument, and the color of many of its bas-reliefs is still intact.

Cartouche with Ramesses III's name

18th Dynasty temple

Temple of Ramesses III

Aerial view of the Medinet Habu area

Rarely included in tours and visited only by a few enthusiasts and specialists, the arresting Temple of Ramesses III at Medinet Habu is the largest and also best-preserved royal cult temple in Thebes that has survived to our time. In antiquity, the site of Medinet Habu (a modern place-name of uncertain origin that means "city of Habu") was called *Tjamet*, and the ancient Egyptians believed it was the place where the god Amun first appeared and where the eight primeval divinities in the so-called *Ogdoad* were buried. During the 20th Dynasty, Medinet

The migdol, *a fortified gateway that gives access to the Medinet Habu complex*

Habu also became the administrative center of all West Thebes. The complex continued to grow until the Graeco-Roman period, and the Coptic city of *Djeme* rose up in this area in a later age. Besides the Temple of Ramesses III, the sacred precinct includes the complex of the Chapels of the God's Wives of Amun of the 25th and 26th Dynasty, and the so-called Temple of the 18th Dynasty or "little temple," begun during the age of Hatshepsut and Tuthmosis III. Access to the precinct is gained by passing through a massive tower modelled after the fortified towers in Asia Minor called *migdol*, or "fortress." Beyond this structure there are, at left, the Chapels of the God's Wives of Amun, and on the right, the Temple of the 18th Dynasty, while opposite it is the majestic first pylon of the Temple of Ramesses III, which was once called "Temple of User-Maat-Re Meryamun

Pylon I of the Temple of Ramesses III is 63 meters long and on average 20 meters high

United with Eternity in the Possession of Amun in West Thebes." The pylon is decorated with scenes of ritual massacres

of enemies on the part of the king in the presence of Amun-Re and Re-Herakhty. In the western part of the south quay of

Plan of the Medinet Habu complex

The hypostyle halls

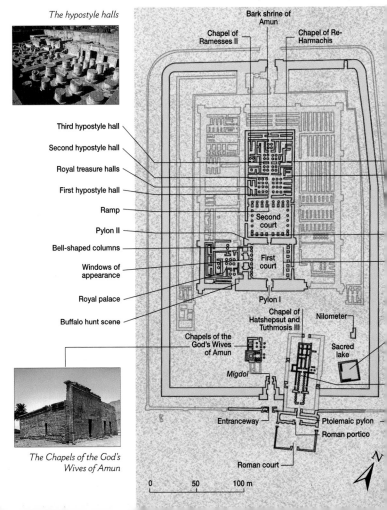

The Chapels of the God's Wives of Amun

One of the papyrus columns with closed capitals in the second court

Scenes of battles against Sea Peoples

Chapels dedicated to various gods and to the deified Ramesses III

Portico with Osirian pillars

Osirian pillars

The sacred lake

Temple of the 18th Dynasty

The Ptolemaic pylon

the pylon there is a splendid bas-relief depicting a buffalo hunt in the marshes.

The side walls of the temple are completely covered with bas-reliefs that take up a surface area of over 7,000 square meters. The ones on the northern side are particularly interesting: they illustrate the battles waged against the Sea Peoples, a motif repeated in the decoration of the first court, which communicates, via an opening known as the "window of appearances,"

Bas-relief depicting a buffalo hunt in the Nile Delta swamp

of Min and the procession of the sacred barks. Three hypostyle halls, which have many side chapels consecrated to various gods, afford access to the bark shrine of Amun.

THE SEA PEOPLES

In the eighth year of his reign, Ramesses III (1186–1154 BC) had to face the invasion of a coalition of peoples from the Aegean-Mediterranean and Asiatic areas who were called the Sea Peoples. These included the Peleset (Philistines), the Denen (Danaoi), the Akhawash (Acheaens), and the Shekelsh (Siculi). Ramesses succeeded in driving back the enemy, who had invaded Egypt by land as well as sea. His exploits are celebrated on the north wall and in the first court of the temple at Medinet Habu, as well as in the Harris Papyrus, now kept in the British Museum.

with the royal palaces, which is situated on the southern side of the temple.

The second court, the "Court of Feasts," which was transformed into a Coptic church, is surrounded by a peristyle with Osirian colossi, while the bas-reliefs on the walls depict the feasts

The Temple of the 18th Dynasty

Southeast of the main temple is the Small Temple built by Hatshepsut and Tuthmosis II and dedicated to the god Amun. A pylon was added to this edifice during the Ptolemaic age, and the Romans then enlarged it with a portico and a court.

The Ramesseum

*T*he memorial temple of Ramesses II, which Champollion called the "Ramesseum," is perhaps the most captivating and elegant monument in West Thebes.

Bust of the "Younger Memnon," which was removed in 1816 by Giovanni Belzoni and is now in the British Museum

The west portico, with the Osirian pillars and hypostyle hall

A lthough it has been victim to the ravages of time and of man, the Ramesseum, which Champollion said was "most noble and pure in Thebes," is extraordinarily fascinating. The temple, called *Memnonion* by the ancient Greek geographer Strabo,

Lower part of the the "Younger Memnon" statue

Remains of royal palace

Colossal bust of Ramesses II, "Sun of Princes"

Pylon I

First court

Pylon II

Present-day entrance

Remains of the temple of the pharaoh's mother Tuya and his consort Nefertari

comprised two pylons, two courts, a hypostyle hall with 48 papyriform columns, and three halls that preceded the sanctuary. The present-day entrance is on the north side of the second court, which lies between two porticos, both of which are decorated with four large statues, the so-called Osirian colossi. These

Second colossal head of Ramesses II

The colossal bust of Ramesses II, "Sun of Princes"

the Battle of Qadesh, waged in Syria by Ramesses against the Hittites in the fifth year of his reign (1275 BC). Next to the ruins of this pylon,

View of the hypostyle hall, with its large papyriform columns

statues portray the pharaoh in the guise of the god Osiris and border the eastern and western sides of the court. It was here that the Italian explorer remaining part of pylon II is the north quay, on the west side of which is a beautiful representation of

View of the Ramesseum and its complex, which has a surface area of over 15,000 square meters

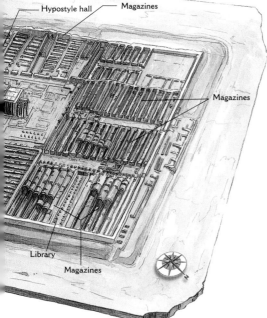

— Second court
— Hypostyle hall
Magazines
Magazines
Library
Magazines

lying in splendor on the ground, is the colossal bust of Ramesses "the Sun of Princes," which was originally 16 meters tall and stood in front of the south quay of pylon II, flanked to the right by another colossus portraying the pharaoh's mother Tuya. A temple on the northern side of the Ramesseum is dedicated to Tuya and Nefertari. On the northern, southern, and western sides of the temple are the remains of the many magazines, which were made of mud bricks and had vaulted ceilings.

Detail of the Battle of Qadesh on the north quay of pylon II

Giovanni Belzoni removed the colossal bust of Ramesses II—known as the "Younger Memnon"—which is 2.67 meters tall; the lower part of the statue, 3 meters long, is still in the court. The only

The Deir al-Bahari Complex

Queen Hatshepsut built a grandiose temple in a valley that the ancient Egyptians considered sacred to the goddess Hathor.

Painted limestone head of Queen Hatshepsut (Egyptian Museum, Cairo)

*The Temple of Hatshepsut (**A**) and, in the background, the Temple of Nebhepetra Mentuhotep (**B**)*

Deir al-Bahari is rarely mentioned by the 19th-century travelers who, on the other hand, give detailed descriptions of the Ramesseum and the temples at Medinet Habu. This is due to the fact that at that time Deir al-Bahari was only an enormous heap of rubble on which a Coptic monastery

Nebhepetra Mentuhotep (Egyptian Museum, Cairo)

had been built. This edifice, which no longer exists, gave its name to the site, since Deir al-Bahari means "north monastery." It was only in 1858 that the first digs carried out by Auguste Mariette brought to light the structures of the mortuary temple of Queen Hatshepsut. Other digs effected in 1891 by Edouard Naville and in 1931 by Herbert Winlock and Emile Baraize, unearthed the most ancient temple built in this area, the work of Nebhepetra Mentuhotep, also known as

Mentuhotep II, the founder of the 11th Dynasty. Excavations were resumed in 1961 by the Polish-Egyptian Mission, which uncovered the site as we see it today and also discovered a third temple built by Tuthmosis III.

Statue of Tuthmosis III from his temple at Deir al-Bahari

The Temple of Hatshepsut

The great architect Senenmut designed the mortuary temple of Hatshepsut, which in ancient times was called *djeser djeseru*, the "sacred of sacreds." It consists of three terraces on different levels that end with the rock-cut sanctuary of Amun, to whom this temple was dedicated, together with Re-Herakhty.

Reconstruction of the temples at Deir al-Bahari

Plan of the Temple of Hatshepsut

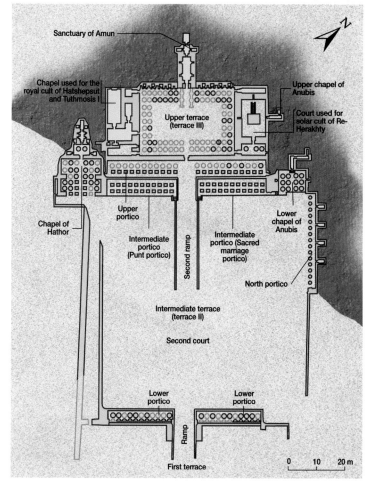

The Punt portico

The Punt Portico

The so-called Punt portico, situated in the southern part of the intermediate portico/colonnade that closes off the second terrace, is perhaps, together with the adjacent Chapel of Hathor, the most visited part of the Temple of Hatshepsut. The bas-reliefs on this portico illustrate an expedition that went to the land of Punt during Hatshepsut's reign. The main purpose of the expedition—which consisted of five ships with 30 rowers each—was to obtain incense, myrrh, and precious wood. The ancient texts tell us that 31 myrrh trees reached Egypt in good enough condition to be transplanted in the Temple of Karnak. Myrrh, a resinous substance produced by a plant of the *Commiphora* genus and considered, among other things, sacred to the god Amun, was used in the embalming process and as a medicine in ancient Egypt, while the incense, a secretion of another plant of the *Boswellia* genus, was used for liturgical fumigations.

THE MYSTERIOUS LAND OF PUNT

Nothing certain is known about the location of the land of Punt, also called "land of the god," where the Egyptians had sent expeditions as early as the 5th Dynasty, during the reign of Sahure, to procure myrrh (antyu) and incense (senetjer), fragrant wood, spices, and quality pelts. With our knowledge of Egyptian nautical technology we can surmise that Punt was located along the coasts of the Red Sea between southern Sudan and Ethiopia. Tuthmosis III and Ramesses III also organized expeditions to Punt.

Hieroglyphs of the place-name "Punt"

Parehu, king of Punt, and his consort Ity, in a bas-relief discovered in 1858 by Mariette and now in the Egyptian Museum, Cairo

Probable location of the land of Punt

Cape Guardafui

Egyptian sailors loading small myrrh trees aboard their ship to be taken to Egypt

The fauna that still lives in the waters of the Red Sea and the Nile is illustrated in the Punt portico bas-reliefs: a perch (genus Tilapia, **A**), a batfish (genus Platax, **B**), a grouper (family Serranidae, C), and a turtle (genus Trionyx, **D**)

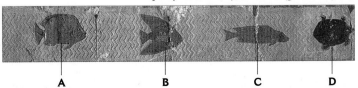

A   B   C   D

The Chapel of Hathor

The Chapel of Hathor

The chapel of Hathor lies immediately south of the Punt portico, which now affords access to the chapel which originally had an independent entrance that opened onto the second terrace.

This chapel consists of a vestibule with six Hathoric pillars and eight columns and a hypostyle hall with 12 columns with Hathoric capitals. This is followed by the rock-hewn sanctuary itself (which is not open to the public), where the most secret ceremonies of

the cult of Hathor took place. The walls of the vestibule and the hypostyle hall are decorated with large multi-colored bas-reliefs depicting the goddess Hathor in the guise of a cow and, on the northern side, the representation of a grandiose naval procession in honor of the goddess

The goddess Hathor in the guise of a cow

accompanied by the queen's soldiers marching in a long parade.

Bas-relief in the Chapel of Hathor depicting Queen Hatshepsut's soldiers in a boat procession in honor of the goddess

The Chapel of Anubis

This chapel is situated in a symmetrical position opposite the Chapel of Hathor at the northern tip of the middle portico, on the walls of which are scenes (not clearly seen) of the divine birth of the queen generated by Amun, who is depicted with the features of Hatshepsut's father, Tuthmosis I. The chapel of Anubis also consists of a hypostyle hall with 12 fluted columns supporting an astronomical ceiling, and a rock-cut sanctuary that is not open to the

public. The hypostyle hall is decorated with offering scenes whose original colors are almost perfectly intact.

The god Anubis with a jackal's head

Hypostyle hall of the Chapel of Anubis

The Temple of Sethos I

*T*he mortuary temple of Sethos I is the northernmost temple in West Thebes. Although many of its structures, built of mud bricks, have been irreparably damaged, its loveliest elements, such as the portico and hypostyle, are in a good state of preservation.

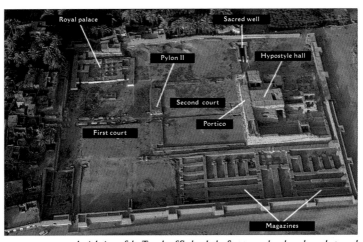

Royal palace   Sacred well   Pylon II   Hypostyle hall   Second court   Portico   First court   Magazines

Aerial view of the Temple of Sethos I; the first two pylons have been destroyed

Present-day visitors to the Temple of Sethos I will find it difficult to imagine what this elegant monument—often called the "Temple of Qurna"—really looked like. Indeed, as in the case of the Temple of Amenophis III, the structures made of mud brick have not resisted the ravages of time. There are only traces of the two large pylons that preceded the portico and most of them can be seen only in an aerial view. Furthermore, up to the 18th century the entire site was used by locals as a quarry for building material. But despite this, what remains is enough to render the elegance of this edifice, which was called "Glorious Sethos in the West of Thebes" and was completed by Ramesses II, the son of Sethos I. The temple was originally surrounded by a massive enclosure wall with numerous towers, which made it look like a fortress, and has been

The portico of the temple that precedes the hypostyle hall

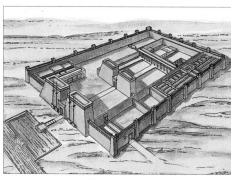

Reconstruction of the Temple of Sethos I

The southern section of the portico affords access to a chapel dedicated to the god Amun and to Ramesses I, the father of Sethos I, whose brief reign did not allow him to build his own mortuary temple. The northeastern part of the portico leads, by means of a wide portal, to a court dedicated to the solar cult of Amun-Re. On the northern side of the temple are the remains of the temple magazines, which are laid out much like those in the

almost totally reconstructed. Once past the present-day entrance, one enters what was the second court, bordered to the west by a majestic portico, which is still well preserved. This portico, supported today by nine bundle columns with papyriform capitals, gives

access, in its central section, to a hypostyle hall with six papyriform columns on the sides of which are six shrines.

Plan of the Temple of Sethos I

The portal leading to the sun court

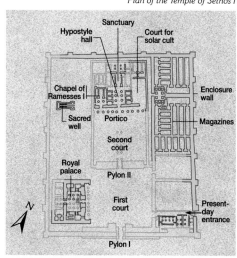

Bas-relief of Amun's sacred bark

Ramesseum, while in the western area are a sacred well and the ruins of the royal palace, a structure which is the first example of this kind of building in an Egyptian temple. The entire Temple of Sethos I complex is being studied and restored by the German Archaeological Institute.

The Luxor Museum

*B*uilt along the Nile, this small but elegant museum contains important archaeological finds from the Theban region and some masterpieces of ancient Egyptian art.

Façade of the Luxor museum, which faces the Nile

Nile (⇨ **28**); a lovely statue of the god Amun with Tutankhamun's features which came from the cache discovered north of pylon VII of the Temple of Karnak (⇨ **20**); a cow that was part of the treasure in the tomb of

The Luxor Museum of Ancient Egyptian Art is located about one kilometer north of the Temple of Luxor, on the road that skirts the Nile and leads to Karnak. This museum, designed by the Egyptian architect Mahmud al-Hakim, was inaugurated in 1975 and houses some masterpieces of

Egyptian sculpture found during the digs carried out in the Thebes area. In 1990 a large underground hall was added to the museum, and the magnificent statues found in 1989 in the cachette of Luxor temple were put on exhibit. The museum is rectangular and has two stories. The upper one contains many finds, including a colossal head of Amenophis III from the mortuary temple of the pharaoh on the west bank of the

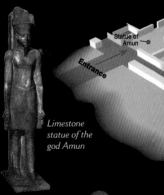

Limestone statue of the god Amun

Statue of Amun

Entrance

The head of a god in the guise of a cow found in Tutankhamun's tomb

Colossal head of Amenophis III

The splendid statue of Tuthmosis III is one of the most important pieces in the museum

Tutankhamun; a greywacke statue of Tuthmosis III that was also

found in the pylon VII cache; and an impressive calcite sculpture group portraying Amenophis III and the crocodile god Sobek that was usurped by Ramesses II and discovered in 1967 at the bottom of a canal near the village of Armant on the west bank of the Nile. A broad staircase goes from the lower floor of the museum to the underground hall dedicated to the statues discovered in 1989 in the Temple of Luxor (⇨ 13). In the back of this hall is the most important find in the cachette, the large quartzite state of Amenophis III, which is 2.45 meters tall

Amenophis III and the crocodile god Sobek

and stands on the sled used to transport it. Among the other finds (which totaled 22 pieces), the most interesting are the diorite statue of

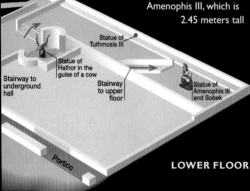

Statue of Tuthmosis III

Statue of Hathor in the guise of a cow

Stairway to underground hall

Stairway to upper floor

Statue of Amenophis III and Sobek

Portico

LOWER FLOOR

View of the room built to house the statues found in the "cachette" of the Temple of Luxor in 1989; in the middle is the quartzite statue of Amenophis III

Statue of the goddess Hathor, also found in the Temple of Luxor

Hathor, the statue of the goddess Iunit, a large headless cobra with the cartouches of the Ethiopian pharaoh Taharqa, and a sculpture group of the pharaoh Haremheb before the god Aten.

Detail of the quartzite statue of Amenophis III

The upper floor has other very important finds: the red granite head of Senusret III discovered in 1970 in front of pylon IV of the Temple of Karnak; and the statue of Amenhotep, Son of Hapu, one of the most famous officials in the court of Amenophis III

Statue of Amenhotep, Son of Hapu

Osirian sandstone statue of Amenophis IV that followed the canons typical of the Amarna art style. And it was precisely the reign of Amenophis IV (who later changed his name to Akhenaten) that produced the most famous and important find

Head of Senusret III

and the architect of his most important royal monuments, who is represented in the dress of a scribe. This latter statue, sculpted in black granite, was found in 1913 in front of pylon X of the Temple of Karnak. Karnak also yielded a Osirian painted limestone pillar portraying the pharaoh Senusret I, as well as an

Pillar of Senusret I in the guise of the god Osiris

Lid of a canopic jar with the head of Queen Tuya, mother of Ramesses II

corresponded to about three handbreadths. These blocks, which on an average measure 54 x 24 x 20 centimeters,

were originally part of the *Gem-pa-aten*, the Temple of Aten that Amenophis IV had built at Karnak. This edifice, east of the portal of Nectanebo, was later dismantled and the decorated blocks were used as filling material inside pylon IX, where in 1968–69 about 40,000 of them were found almost wholly intact. These *talatats* were studied, and the most beautiful ones were reassembled in their

in the entire museum: the so-called talatat wall, which takes up most of the wall space on the upper floor. This wall is seventeen meters long, three meters high, and is made up of 283 sandstone blocks elegantly decorated with multicolored bas-reliefs which the Arab workmen called *talatat*, from the word *talata*, which means "three," perhaps because their length and height

Statue of Amenophis IV-Akhenaten

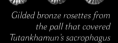

Gilded bronze rosettes from the pall that covered Tutankhamun's sarcophagus

original position inside the museum. They are the only existing example of decoration of a temple of Aten. The scenes on the left-hand part of the wall

received the sun's rays, each of which ends with a hieroglyph of the "vital breath." In the right-hand section of the wall most of the scenes regard the daily life of workmen and artisans who worked on the temple. Among the other finds on this floor is a series of 63 gilded bronze rosettes that were part of a much larger group (637 pieces) inserted in the pall which covered the sarcophagus of Tutankhamun, and the elegant calcite lid of a canopic jar with the features of Queen Tuya, the consort of Sethos I and mother of

UPPER FLOOR

Central showcase

Talatat wall

represent adoration of the god Aten on the part of Amenophis, who thus

Ramesses II, which was found in 1972 in Tomb 80 in the Valley of the Queens.

Reconstruction of the wall of talatats, *an Arabic word for these blocks of sculpted sandstone from the dismantled Temple of Aten in Karnak that were found inside pylon IX. This is considered the most important find in the museum*

The Mummification Museum

Inaugurated in 1998, the Mummification Museum of Luxor provides visitors with an overall picture of this procedure and the rituals connected to it, which are some of the most famous and well-known aspects of ancient Egyptian civilization.

A dim, suffused light evokes the sepulchral atmosphere in which the finds were discovered

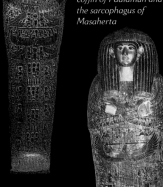

The Luxor Mummification Museum, situated on the bank of the Nile a few hundred meters north of the Temple of Luxor, was opened in 1997. It consists of a large underground hall that is immersed in dim half-light that was skillfully created by the Egyptian architect Gamal Bakry, who also designed the museum, in order to recreate a sepulchral atmosphere. The central core of the exhibition comprises the beautiful and richly decorated coffin of Padiamun,

The anthropoid coffin of Padiamun and the sarcophagus of Masaherta

high priest of Amun, who lived in the 21st Dynasty, and the sarcophagus of Masaherta, another high priest of Amun. His sarcophagus, found with his mummy still inside, was discovered in a perfect state of preservation. All around these displays are the objects connected with the complicated embalming procedure and the magic ritual that accompanied it: chisels, pincers, scalpels, and spatulas. Then there were canopic jars, containers generally made of alabaster that were placed under the protection of four mummiform genii, the

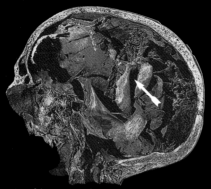

A section of the cranium of a mummy with a mass of bitumen (indicated by the arrow) placed there by the embalmers

Egypt, that was dominated by Osiris, Lord of the Afterlife, the goddesses Isis and Nephthys, and Anubis, the god with a dog's head who was considered the discoverer of embalming. The exhibition is rounded off with some animal mummies, including the ibis, crocodile, ram, and cat, which were sacred respectively to the god Thoth, the lord of writing and magic, the god Sobek, the god Amun, who ruled the pantheon of Theban divinities, and the goddess Bastet.

children of Horus and Isis, called Amset, Hapi, Duamutef, and Qebehsennuf, whose images were represented on the stopper of the jars, which contained the liver, stomach, intestine, and lungs of the deceased, while the heart, considered the seat of thought and

One of the four canopic jars used to preserve the viscera of the deceased. The falcon-head lid represents Qebehsennuf

Mummy of a cat

the soul, was left in the deceased's body.
There are also many *ushabti*, the magic statuettes that were placed in

the tomb so that the deceased could call them back to life by means of magic formulas and could carry out the most difficult tasks in the afterlife.
The museum has the implements used during the Opening of the Mouth Ceremony during which the priest uttered special formulas and thus magically revived the deceased's vital functions. On display are the most important of the numerous amulets that were placed on the mummy to protect it magically (more than a hundred were found on the mummy of Tutankhamun), as well as wooden statuettes of the major deities of the mortuary world of ancient

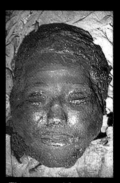

This uncovered face of a late epoch mummy shows the exceptional state of preservation achieved

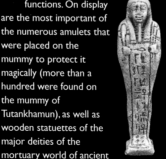

An ushabti, *a magic statuette placed in the tomb to aid the deceased*

Mummy of a large Nile crocodile, an animal sacred to the god Sobek

The Temple of Dendera

Situated on the west bank of the Nile, about 60 kilometers north of Luxor, the Temple of Hathor at Dendera is one of the masterpieces of Ptolemaic architecture.

Column capital with portraits of the goddess Hathor

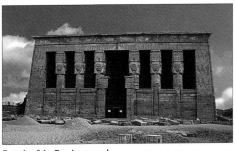

Façade of the Dendera temple

certain—July 16, 54 BC, during the reign of Ptolemy XII Neos Dionysos, the father of Cleopatra—while the Osirian chapels were inaugurated a few years afterward, on December

Temple of the birth of Isis

Kiosk for the statue of the *ba* of Hathor

Terrace

Chapel of the zodiac

Sacred lake

Hypostyle hall

Bark shrine

Entrance to the Temple of Hathor

The present-day site of Dendera was once the home of ancient Iunet, the center of the cult of the goddess Hathor up to the Middle Kingdom. Later on, during the Graeco-Roman period, it was the site of the city *Tentyris*, the main temple of which was dedicated to Hathor, her consort Horus, and their child Ihy. The temple at Dendera is the only Egyptian temple the foundation date of which is known for

The famous zodiac at Dendera

28, 47 BC. Such precision is due to the fact that a famous zodiac was carved on the ceiling of one of the chapels: a study of the conjuction of the stars represented on it allowed scholars to determine the dates exactly. The zodiac

The majestic hypostyle *hall in the Dendera temple*

astronomic ceiling of which, 17 meters high, is supported by 18 large columns with Hathoric capitals on which the goddess is represented with cow's ears. The temple, on a North-South axis, includes a series of chapels laid out around the central sanctuary, regenerating her energy. Immediately north of the Temple of Hathor is a large Roman age *mammisi* or birth house dating from Augustus' time, in which the birth of Hathor's son Ihy was celebrated. On the columns of the *mammisi* are many portraits of the god Bes, who was

was removed in 1823 and sold to the Louvre museum in Paris, while a plaster cast has replaced it in the chapel.

The temple of Dendera, a veritable gem of Ptolemaic architecture, is decorated with highly elegant bas-reliefs, many of which have preserved their original colors.

The Roman mammisi of the Dendera temple

some deep crypts in which the temple treasure was stored, and the statue of the *ba* of Hathor which, on occasion of

connected with the birth cult. Next to the Roman birth house is a smaller one dating from Nectanebo I's reign, the *Sanatorium*, a sort of hospital in which the priests cared for the ill according to instructions they received from Hathor herself, and the remains of a 5th-century Christian basilica.

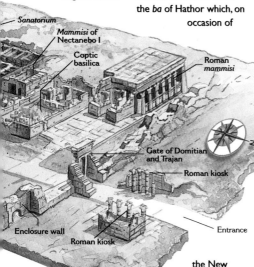

Sanatorium
Mammisi of Nectanebo I
Coptic basilica
Roman mammisi
Gate of Domitian and Trajan
Roman kiosk
Enclosure wall
Roman kiosk
Entrance

The god Bes

The edifice is famous for the beauty of its *pronaos* or outer hypostyle hall, the

the New Year's festival, was transported to the special chapel on the terrace to be exposed to the sun's rays, thus

ESSENTIAL BIBLIOGRAPHY

Baines, J., J. Malek, *Atlas of Ancient Egypt*, Oxford and New York, 1980.

Barguet, P., *Le temple d'Amon-Rê à Karnak. Essai d'exégèse*, Le Caire, 1962.

Clayton, P.A., *Chronicle of the Pharaohs*, London, 1994.

Golvin, J.C., J.C. Goyon, *Les bâtisseurs de Karnak*, Paris, 1987.

Grandet, P., *Ramsés III, Histoire d'un règne*, Paris, 1993.

Lauffray, J., *Karnak d'Égypte, domaine du divin*, Paris, 1979.

Lipinska, J., *Deir el-Bahari. The Temple of Thutmosis III*, Warsaw, 1977.

Naville, E., *The Temple of Deir el Bahari*, London, 1894-1908.

Porter, B., R.L.B. Moss. *Topographical Bibliography of Ancient Egyptian Hieroglyphic Texts, Reliefs and Paintings*. Vol.II, Oxford, 1964.

Siliotti, A. *Egypt—Temples, Men, and Gods*, Cairo, 2001.

Siliotti, A. *Guide to the Valley of the Kings*, Vercelli, 1996.

Siliotti, A. *The Discovery of Ancient Egypt*, Vercelli, 1998.

Wilkinson, R.H., *The Complete Temples of Ancient Egypt*, London, 2000.

DRAWINGS

Stefania Cossu pages 4, 35 above, 36.

Melissa Frigotto pages 10-11, 18-19, 23, 26-27, 32-33, 46-47.

Jean Claude Golvin/Errance Éd. pages 6-7, 39 above.

Lucia Grassi pages 13, 15.

Stefano Trainito pages 40-41; 42-43.